LESSONS MY FATHER TAUGHT ME....

**"Whatever Job or Position You're in,
Be an Asset"**

Yvette Hebert

(Lessons My Father Taught Me)
Copyright © 2018 by (Yvette Hebert)

ISBN: 978-1-5136-3270-4

Available on
Amazon and Kindle

Presented to

____

By

____

Date

____

Dedication

This book is dedicated to my parents and my brother; may they rest in peace. My father on earth and in Heaven taught me valuable lessons about life that have made me to become the person I am today. They taught me how to save, budget my money, moral and values. Mom taught me to always shine and take center stage while being the best at whatever I do. I was taught to endure through all things and never give up, to be the best at everything that I do in life.

My father told me that if I fall, I have to get back up and do better the next time. They taught me that no matter how many times I fall, I would never fail if I didn't give up. They taught me to never ever let anyone abuse me without outthinking them to victory. They taught me to work with my mind, instead of my emotions and feelings. My father taught me to be a forward thinker always; to prepare for the worst, but focus on the win! My Brother showed me how to survive in the wilderness, how to protect myself, and how to do and fix things.

Most importantly, they taught me to love GOD, to never lose my faith, and to believe in the impossible!

I love you all with all my heart! The lessons I learned are very close to my heart and will never be forgotten.

Acknowledgement

Inspired by "MY SON"

To my son, this book will be the family treasure for years to come, written to inspire you and future generations.
Your inspiration and determination, gave me the confidence to share my story. You are a man of faith and courage, I am so proud of you! Make wise decisions and sacrifice for the win!
The first book written in our family a short read, but powerful one! Remember the family lessons and pass them on... It only takes one person to make a change,
be that one!
I love you with all my heart! Mom

Contents

Introduction

This book was written to inspire others to be the best that they can be at whatever it is that they do in life.

I realized that I have a lot of experiences on this earth and that I should share my experiences with the world because it may help someone else understand how things work and be inspired and motivated to change the world, one step at a time.

Everything we encounter in life is a lesson. The question is do we learn from them and take a stand to make a difference in our own life. "Do we dare to do what others won't, so we can dare to be what others won't be!" Selah...

Chapter 1

I WOULD LIKE TO tell you my story. When I got out of high school, I had no idea what I wanted to be or what I even wanted to do with life, but I knew I had to do something because I knew that with the life I was living, I was most likely going to end up dead.

I realized that the people I associated with weren't going anywhere in life and I did not plan on having that lifestyle of living and going nowhere. So, I started limiting myself to the people that I associated with; backing away slowly, not dissing anybody, not being mean to anybody, but whenever they called me and said, "Hey Yvette, do you want to go this party?" I would say, "Ahh!!! Nah man, I have to go to work."

After high school, I went straight to trade school and got a job. I started in the medical field and took a ten-month course to become an E.K.G. tech, which is basically a heart tech. After I graduated, I started working in a hospital.

Now while working, I grew to become the best version of me. Let me explain how I grew in that field of work and the sacrifices that I made in order to get to that point. I sacrificed hanging out, I sacrificed smoking marijuana because all I did was sleep and I felt it was just eating away my brain cells because I would just sleep for hours. I also started to have memory loss; I couldn't remember anything.

I soon realized that, natural or not, marijuana was damaging my brain, and so I decided I didn't want to be bothered by it. Instead, I switched to cigarettes because they didn't change my mental state, only my physical state. That's a new one; a great excuse to ruin my lungs, right? I know, and still today, I wonder what the heck I was thinking. Of course, every now and then I did go somewhere, but I had done a lot of partying in my high school years, so when I got out of high school, I was done with that. It was like it wasn't exciting to me anymore because I was growing up. It was time to grow up and be an adult; it was time to take responsibility for my life. I had no time for trivialities because I was working full-time, my check was coming in, and it was coming in regularly. So when my friends called me to go hang out, I had no time for that because I was totally focused on my job.

So when I lived with my parents, I paid rent to my dad, and when I moved out of my parents' house at the age of nineteen, he gave me a check for five thousand dollars, and I asked, "What is this?" My dad replied, "This is the rent that you've been paying me."

Now, reminding me, I had been paying rent since I got my first job at sixteen; I was paying rent because my dad was teaching me responsibility, he was showing me how to be a woman, how to grow up, and how to handle my own business. So you can imagine how I felt when I was getting ready to move out and he handed me a check for five thousand dollars.

My dad sat me down, and he said, "Yvette, here's all the rent that you paid us; we didn't need your money."

I felt stupid because I was fussing and arguing and complaining because I had to pay rent, "Why do I have to pay rent to my parents? Ugghhh…. Why do I have to pay rent?"

I didn't realize it at the time, but that's what parents are for, to teach us! I gave them the rent money, and they saved it so they could teach me how to save and be able to pay bills on time. They were teaching me a great lesson, and I didn't know it until I was moving out.

So my dad said, "Yvette, here's a check for five thousand dollars. Now, you work every day, right?" "Yes," I replied. "Okay, put this five thousand dollars in a savings account and don't touch it no matter what; live off of your work pay. Take twenty percent of your check and add to that five thousand every month. The other eighty percent, pay your rent, pay your car note, pay your car insurance, and pay your household bills, okay?"

He continued, "And you don't touch that money; the only reason that you touch that money is if you're about to get kicked out of your house and you lost your job, or you need food while not working. It's a security blanket, that's what it's there for; it's for emergencies only. Understand? Going to the mall, and buying clothes is not an emergency."

He continued, "An emergency is not buying some new shoes. You already have ten pair of shoes, maybe even more, why do you need more shoes? They're in good shape, be grateful for what you have. Buying shoes is not an emergency; that's not even a priority, that's the mind of a poor person, they buy things, and don't have money to pay their bills when something arises, they are not prepared for it, they live paycheck to paycheck. A poor person mentality, is a person that will go out and spend every dime they have and they won't have any money left at the end of their paycheck." My dad continued, "There are people in this world that made only one hundred fifty dollars a week and have become millionaires; there are people that have made twenty thousand dollars a year and have become millionaires off of twenty thousand dollars a year. How did they do that? They did that because of their sacrifice; they didn't go out and eat every day, they went out to the grocery store and bought a specific list of groceries for the month or for the week, and they stuck to that, and they made their meals. Of course, they took themselves out for a treat, and they went on a vacation, but they had allocated a savings account for that vacation, maybe they put twenty dollars a month in a container for the vacation. When you sacrifice, all you need money for is your essentials; gas, food, and rent."

Chapter 2

MY DAD BELIEVED In the virtue of work, and as a young person, I worked a lot. My dad really believed in just spending money on gas, food, and rent.

So, my dad advised me, "All you need money for, you need a full tank of gas every week, and then you need maybe two dollars a day, in case you want to get some snacks at work because you will pack a lunch and take it with you to work. He was like, every now and then, once a week, you could buy yourself a lunch, a meal or you can take yourself out to dinner, occasionally, not all the time but you get to spend a minimum of two dollars a day.

So you save from your own weekly allowance to go on that dinner or lunch date, you will sacrifice those snacks for that meal."

As for gas, back then, you could fill up your tank for like twenty dollars, if not less. So, twenty dollars and then two dollars a day makes thirty-four dollars a week, right? And thirty-four dollars a week is a hundred and thirty-six dollars a month, was what I was allocated to spend monthly as one of my expenses.

Now, if I really wanted to save, I didn't have to spend that two dollars a day because I could go to the store and I could buy groceries, and I could take my snacks, right? So, I decided I was just going to stick with the twenty dollars a week for gas because I'd need gas for my car and food for my body. So, buying gas for my car and food would cost me how much?

For food, at two dollars a day times thirty, I would spend a total of sixty dollars a month.

But I didn't spend the whole sixty dollars. I would spend just ten and refuse to get a snack that wouldn't have made me a dime.

I would carry ten dollars around with me in my pocket and put the other fifty in my savings account, with the money that he had given me in the check.

This amounted to only fifty dollars a month, but it was something. I wasn't a big shopper, and even though I liked nice things, I was simply sacrificing to achieve my goals.

So, what were my goals? What were my dreams? I didn't know exactly, but I knew I needed money to make it happen when the idea came to me, so I made the sacrifice so I wouldn't have too much of a struggle when the idea came to me.

Let me ask you; that five-dollar cup of Starbucks coffee that you're drinking, man, how many times do you drink that in a week? Do you know how much that is costing you per month?

You might not realize it until you are faced with a situation in your life that's an emergency (unfair traffic ticket, due a refund and they won't refund you), and you need the advice of an attorney and you don't have the money to pay the attorney. Now you're going to take a loss when you could have gotten an attorney for less than twenty dollars a MONTH, but you were easily spending thirty dollars a WEEK on one cup of coffee. You need insurance to protect your hard earned money.

We need to get our priorities right. What are priorities? Priorities are the things that make the rich, rich and the poor, poor. Because of this simple reason, we need to get our priorities in order. Most people won't pay for car insurance, but have all the latest shoes, clothes, etc. Then they just complain when things happen, and they could have avoided it in the first place, if only they had made the sacrifice.

Have you ever heard your mom say, "I have no money for that," when you knew she had some money?

I used to be quick to say, "Mom, I know you have some money," and she would reiterate by saying, "I don't have money for that."

What she was really teaching me, in essence, was, "I don't have money to waste; my money is an investment."

My mom was a hustler; she was a true entrepreneur. I didn't realize that until my late years recently that I was like her.

My mom sold Avon, Tupperware, Crystal, and pretty much everything else. She also made a variety of dolls and statues.

I got my spirit of entrepreneurship from my mother, but I never thought about it, at least, not consciously. Not until I   learned about MLMs and Network Marketing, that's when I realized that I had an entrepreneur right in front of me my whole life and didn't even know it!

She never took me to the side and taught me what she was doing or why she was doing it. She never educated me on being an entrepreneur; she just sheltered me and gave me things. The truth is, she spoiled me a little... well, a lot. She made all my clothes, so I had one of a kind clothing, I was really blessed, but didn't realize it because I wanted to go shopping, like all the other kids, but my clothes were made so much better than what the stores had. Of course, we don't understand these things until we get older, but the clothes were one of a kind, and she saved tons of money making them. I would say, I had a pretty smart mom with a lot of talent.

So, I didn't realize what she did with the Avon and Crystal other than take orders, but I knew I had something in me, and I wouldn't be working a job for long. When I grew up, I was too inquisitive, and had that entrepreneur spirit in me. My mom thought she was just saving and making extra money. She always wanted us to have a better life than her, and wanted me to go to school and become something great. She didn't understand what she had created in me, but I was going to be something great without the college degree. I remember when I was about 10 or 11, I would have talent shows in the backyard when my parents were at work, and we were off school. I would interview all the kids on what their talents were and told them we were going to perform and charge all the other kids 10 cents to get in. Haha, I even went up to .25 cents after I got good at it. I had a lemonade stand too; I would say I started off pretty young as an Entrepreneur.

My mom took her sewing skills and made money making everyone's ballet costumes, so her cost was FREE for me to take ballet, tap, and jazz, and she charged to make all the costumes for others. Yep, my mom was brilliant, I would say so myself. However, to her, she was just surviving, but to me, I would say she set the stage for me.

Lessons my father taught me....

Chapter 3

I READ BOOKS ALL the time. I would read and read, but I never read drama. I read books that were going to educate my mind. If it was teaching me something about how to be a business owner, I was reading that book. I was so smart everybody kept saying things like, "You should be a lawyer" because I knew how to break it down and still do.

I don't want to be boastful, but I was smart, and I was smart because I educated myself. I have come to realize that there's no wisdom, knowledge or growth without education. Whether you're self-educated or you go to school to get educated, it doesn't matter.

I happened to go to college, and I took a few courses. But I only took courses to learn what I needed to know. For example, I took accounting courses because I needed to know how to do my books. I took a typing class because computers were coming out and I needed to know how to type. I took shorthand because I was doing dictation for myself and I couldn't write as fast as my brain was going, I had to learn a way to write it all down. See, we didn't have computers everywhere back then; we had to write a lot of stuff down by hand. So I had to take shorthand so that I could learn how to write as fast as my thoughts came.

So, back to the sacrifice. You see, there is no mission, no success without the sacrifice. Please hear me when I tell you that there is no success or mission without the sacrifice. There is only a dream that's never going to come to reality; it's just going to wander around in your head, and you will keep wondering why it's not manifesting and why it's not coming to pass, but the simple reason is because you are not sacrificing to get there. So I'm going to step into discussing how to become an asset at your job or in whatever it is that you do and I will illustrate by telling you my personal stories because I have a lot of them. I've been through a lot in my lifetime, and I love that I've been through every challenging experience, from the good to the bad to the worst; from the drama to the sacrifice to everything else in between.

I have been through more than you can imagine and I don't even care to share everything right now because a lot of it happened back then. I will leave the past in the past because I'm moving up and forward, not down and backward.

So the first story I have to tell you on becoming an asset concerns my first job after graduating from medical trade school. Now, I worked in a hospital; I started out as an E.K.G. tech, and along with the job, others had to do some transcribing. This is because the doctors read the E.K.G. and then you have to transcribe it after they dictated with a little Dictaphone.

So When they transcribed, I watched the others and, I would always go, "Oh, let me try that, let me see how that works."

I was extremely inquisitive at the time still am and I really like challenges because if it didn't challenge me, it wouldn't hold my interest. I don't know what they call that these days, maybe A.D.D. Hahaha, but it doesn't matter. It was hard for things to hold my attention because once I learned something, I'd become bored, then have to go and learn something else.

So after learning how to transcribe, I went on to bigger things. I'm not going to go into all the details of it, but I ended up going all the way to the emergency room and being the person that they called when there was a code blue.

Do you know what a code blue is? A cold blue is when somebody is experiencing a cardiac arrest, and they're dying.

I was well known in that hospital facility, and so it was quite common to hear things like, "Oh get Yvette." "Is Yvette on staff now?" or "Get Yvette down here now."

I had a ninety-five percent rate of C.P.R. bringing people back; patients that were dying, literally bringing them back to life.

Was I that good, you may ask? I was that good. Hahaha… and that was because I don't do anything in my life that I wouldn't be great at. If I was going to be a janitor, I was going to mop that floor like I was going to be the best janitor there was. You see?

My ten months in trade school took me further than a four-year degree. One career, fueled by this one ten-month course, I worked this field for five years, from the age of eighteen until the age of twenty-two. I worked in about five hospitals. I went on to work in a recovery facility in Beverly Hills, California, on Sunset Boulevard, with one of the most renowned plastic surgeons in the world today.

He hooked me up to work in a recovery facility where I actually helped patients. So my career grew by leaps and bounds with only ten months of education, but let me tell you how exactly it grew.

Now I didn't just go to work just to work the job they gave me; I learned everybody else's job while there because I was already good at my job. So I would go in, get my job done, and then I'd hang around with somebody else, and ask, "What are you doing? How do you do that?" I was inquisitive!

Chapter 4

SO WHEN THE opportunity arose, I was ready to move on it. When that next position came, when the transcription position became available, guess who stepped in? Me! Did I get a higher pay for that? Absolutely! Let me tell you, not only did I get extra pay but now I was a Cardiology Tech and a Transcriber, so I got a pay raise.

So, guess what? I was so valuable because I was such an asset to my current position. It might have seemed small, but to the entire hospital. I was an asset; I made myself valuable, and when I made myself useful, I was able to give value to the hospital, and that value, guess what it became in return... I got to go to work whenever I felt like it.

Who works in the hospital today and goes to work whenever they feel like it? You know that you have a schedule for that day; you know that you have to show up for that day, right? Yeah, okay, but if you decided that you needed to make a detour, you need to come in a couple of hours late, how many of you could call in and say, "I'm going to be a couple of hours late?" And they'd be like, "Oh!!! Okay cool," because they know that you're going to get your work done once you come in, even when two hours late.

I was so good; my supervisor told me, she was like, "Yvette, you could come in, clock in, leave and come back." How cool is that?

It sure sounded cool but did I do that? No, because it was against my values; to me, that was like stealing from the hospital, and I didn't do that, but I did take advantage of coming in late or leaving early if needed. I could come to work depending on how busy that particular day was, and in two, three hours, all my work would be done.

I would sit there and watch other people leisurely taking eight hours to do their job. But really, why take eight hours to do your job just because you got eight hours? Why not finish up in two or three hours and use those other hours to read a book? These were my thoughts most days, although I have to admit, it depends on what kind of work you do. I worked the night shift, by the way, so it wasn't that busy, but whatever work you do, you want to expand to other areas, you want to know what everybody does because you never know, who knows?

Even till this day, I am very knowledgeable about the different operations that happen in a hospital. Who knows, it may not happen, but I may end up owning a hospital one day. Now I know how to run those departments, right? That's not my dream or my goal, but I'm just saying. What if it was my destiny to do that?

You have to know, you have to learn it, do it, and delegate it. This is exactly what business owners do; they learn how the systems work, they work in the systems, so they make sure that they work, and then they delegate it.

Delegating simply means that they hire somebody else to step in and to do that job for them while they do greater things. You see, did that make sense to everybody? So, it doesn't matter what type of job you do; you want to be an asset at your job. You want your boss to say, "Hey!!! You're good!!!"

And let me tell you, after I worked that job for a while, I ended up getting another job. So, I worked from seven in the morning till three in the afternoon. After my shift at three, I had to be at my other job from three-thirty to eleven-thirty at night, and I had to drive an hour away in between jobs. So, yes, was I late for my next job? Absolutely! Did they care? Absolutely not! Did they fire me? Absolutely not because they knew when I got there, I was going to handle my business, they already knew.

So, I worked two jobs and saved up so much money because I lived by those ground rules that my dad taught me. I put that twenty percent up, I never touched that five thousand dollars because I always kept a job, never touched it, but I only added and added to it.

From the time I was nineteen till the time I turned twenty-three, I had thirty thousand dollars saved up; actually it was a little bit more, closer to about thirty-five thousand I had saved up, okay. So, from five thousand, I grew that to thirty-five thousand dollars. How about that? Because I worked and I saved, I had been able to put away even more than the average person makes in a year, you know....

Chapter 5

SO THAT'S THIRTY-FIVE thousand dollars in just five years. And I didn't even save fifteen thousand dollars a year, remember? Because if I saved fifteen thousand dollars a year, where would I be? At about a seventy-five thousand dollars in the bank.

So, that shows you I did take care of myself a little bit... hahaha, I did spoil myself a little bit, I had a car, I had an apartment. So, when I got my apartment, remember I was moving out of my parents' home, all my furniture was paid for with cash. So, what I'm saying is because I was saving, even though I was paying rent at home, I was able to do that because I had a job since I was sixteen. So, I paid cash for my furniture and my deposit on my apartment.

I went and bought the furniture, and I put it on a lay-a-way plan – back then we had a lay-a-way plan... how many people know about lay-a-way? You go to Kmart, and you buy a bunch of clothes, you put them on layaway and then, you pay a little bit on that bill each check, and eventually, you get your merchandise, right? So, I paid a little bit of money each month until my furniture was paid for and then, once my furniture was paid for, I said, "Hmm, now I need an apartment now."

I didn't know where, didn't know how I was going to get an apartment, but knew I was paying my dad two hundred and fifty dollars a month. I was paying my dad two hundred and fifty dollars a month, maybe and probably gave him a little extra after that, I'm not sure but, you know, based on what I was saving myself, I can't remember that far back, I'm little old now. Hahaha. So, the bottom line is this; I kept saving! I kept saving! I kept saving!

Now, I needed to manifest an apartment, and I knew I was paying my dad two hundred and fifty dollars, so I was like, "Look, I'm comfortable with paying two hundred and fifty dollars, can I get an apartment that's two hundred and fifty dollars?"

There were no apartments going for two hundred and fifty dollars; they were going for like three, four, five hundred dollars, to get you a nice little apartment, right? But, I knew, like I knew that I was going to find an apartment for two hundred and fifty dollars; I didn't know how but I believed I was going to find it and I wasn't tripping. I knew that I was going to get what I asked for because I was so focused on seeing what it was that I wanted that I was going to find it.

So, I was patient, my furniture was about to get out of lay way, I didn't have anywhere to put it yet, but it was okay; I was not stressing because stressing causes you to miss your blessing. If you stress, it causes frustration, frustration causes negative emotions, and everything just goes crazy, you end up sending all this negative energy to the universe, and then the universe sends back negative times, and people are like "When it rains, it storms."

That might be true but what were you putting out there? It's negative energy that causes the storm to hit you so hard. When I was young, I did have a lot of storms, so when they hit, they hit me hard.

I wasn't frightened of the storms, but I was a little frustrated because I didn't understand. I kept thinking, "Dang, look what I told myself, do you know what you were saying to yourself?"

I experienced a lot of this when I was thirteen or fourteen, and I later realized that eventually, karma comes back and it's going to come back when you're doing well. Karma doesn't come back when you're doing bad, karma comes back when you're doing good, and you're like, "Oh my God!!! I can't believe this is happening to me right now."

Of course, you can't, but it's happening because you brought it into existence years before, so you have to work on changing your karmic outcome. You can change it quickly, but some stuff is still going to happen because it's just called life and it depends on how you choose to see it. You can either live your life or you can lose your life, how you interpret it is how you win or lose in life.

So, back to the apartment, I didn't really know how this apartment was going to come. So, one day, my boyfriend – he is my best friend today, but we were dating at the time called me up.

He said, "Hey!!! Yvette, you still looking for a place?"

"Yeah," I replied, "I need an apartment."

"Hey!!! My uncle has a building over here on such and such and such…" he went on, "why don't you come check it out?"

I said, "How much is the rent?"

(Look at God),

He said, "Two fifty."

I said, "I want it no matter where it's at; like I don't care where it's at, I want it."

So we go to this area together, we pulled up, and when I saw the house, it's not like a super, you know, duper great area but it was good enough, it was okay.

There was a huge field, and if you pull into this field, you had to drive down this long dirt road. (This was still in the city, in L.A., in fact). After the dirt road was the apartment, it was like this set of three garages, and there was an apartment over the garage.

I think there were houses in front of an apartment building, at one point. I didn't really know because it was just this big vacant lot now. So I drove back in my new car, worried about my tires getting a flat because I have to drive down this dirt road, but I was like, "Two fifty, I'm in, and I have a garage, I am totally in, right?"

So, just in time, I got my furniture out, and I moved into this apartment, and I loved this apartment! Oh my God!!! I was nineteen; I didn't have to live at home with my parents, you know what I mean, I was just living the life at the same rent I was paying my parents.

In my head, I had thoughts like, "I can find an apartment for what I'm paying my parents for rent; I didn't want to pay them rent."

You know how those snotty-nosed little kids are, I was one of them! Haha!

Chapter 6

SO, I GOT ALL MOVED IN, and I became an adult that day!

Yes, I manifested it, and how did I manifest it? I manifested that apartment because I saw it in my mind, I felt it in my heart, and I knew what it was that I wanted and needed. In the end, the universe and God made it happen automatically because I had believed it was coming, I knew it was coming, and it came. It showed up because I never doubted, I never ever doubted it.

Was I out looking for other apartments? Oh yeah, I was looking, but everything was too expensive.

I was like, "No, that's too much. I can't do that one, that's too much."

You have to understand that I wasn't making a whole lot of money at the time. I only had one job at that time; I got the two jobs later. So I ended up moving into my two hundred and fifty dollar apartment, and it was just phenomenal. I'm still grateful and blessed to this day, that God was able to manifest that. It taught me a lot, and God manifested my first business in the same way.

Now I stayed at this apartment for like four years, I think, and during this period, I saved up a lot of money because my income increased. I was nineteen when I moved into the apartment, and by twenty, I had two jobs. For three years, I had two jobs, and concerning the second job, I just stacked the whole check. I saved it all because my first check was enough to pay rent, pay for my car note, rental insurance, gas, and left a couple of dollars a week for food because I cooked.

Now, when I turned twenty-three, and I was working for this plastic surgeon in Beverly Hills, we were doing a facelift patient once, so I prepped the patient. I was washing her hair and pulling her staples out of her hair and voila!!! A light bulb came up in my head.

I realized I wanted to do hair.

"Hair?!!!" The doctor said after I had told him. "Hair?!!! No, no, no, no, no, you're going to school to get your R.N."

Now, at the time, I was in school taking some college courses because I initially thought I wanted to become an R.N."

I was already very good at what I did, and I really did a lot of things, while working for Doctors – I'm not going to call their names – but I wasn't licensed to do those things. Still, they trusted me so much that they allowed me to do these things. These were all things that a licensed nurse would do, but I was doing them very well because once again, I made myself an asset on my job.

So while I was on the job, originally I was hired as a surgical circulator.

That was my official title although I was inclined to get involved in other things. I always watched the surgeon closely as he performed his operations.

So, while I watched him do surgery, the whole process fascinated me and one day, after surgery, I took the book of surgical instruments that were used to perform the surgery home with me. I didn't even know myself why I took the instrument book home; I was just a curious kid that needed to know everything that she could know because I was naturally like that. I needed to download information into my head, for maybe no other reason than I needed to know so I could take extra steps.

It was at that office that I learned how to do accounting. I knew for sure that the office was being embezzled and so I tried to tell the surgeon, but he didn't understand.

I eventually got to do the books there, and I learned how to do that just by sitting there, watching the secretary do the books. I even questioned her a couple of times because I took that accounting class in school, remember?

I didn't go to college to get a degree, I went to college to take classes for things that I wanted and I needed to know, and most of these were non-credit classes and a couple of credited classes, but I didn't care. If it had the information I needed to learn, I took it; that's what you go to school for if you don't like college.

Chapter 7

SO ONE DAY, the nurse doesn't show up for surgery. On this day, we're doing an upper and lower blepharoplasty, that's your upper and lower eyelids. The same patient was getting a facelift later on this same day.

The nurse does not show up for work that morning, and the doctor is like, "Yvette!"

He's fussing, and he's screaming, and he's mad, and the patient is ready. The anesthesiologist is there, and everybody is ready to get to work, and the nurse is conspicuously absent. Since she hasn't called, we don't know whether she was in an accident or something, we don't have any idea what happened.

And right there, the opportunity came! Wow, how about that? Who was in that office that had taken those surgical instruments out, watched them do surgery every day, knew every medication, every suture, every instrument that was needed to do that procedure? Guess who knew it. Me! I became the number one valued asset for that doctor.

So the doctor says, "Yvette, do you think you can assist me with this surgery?"

I looked, stepped back and smiled; I said, "I don't think I can help. I know I can help, I know what you all do."

In my head, I said, "Only a fool would be here every day and not watch and learn; only a fool doesn't learn. I'm not a fool; I'm a woman of wisdom and knowledge."

So, we got in, and we were all scrubbed up and got gowned up, and we're doing this surgery, and he's doing this upper and lower blepharoplasty, and he's calling out his instruments, and I was like bam!!! Bam!!! Bam!!! Bam!!! As I handed him everything he called out for.

Now, we were scrubbed up, and we were in the surgery room, and he was fussing at me. He was fussing at me because he was mad because the nurse didn't show up, but regardless of the fussing, in the midst of the surgery, he had been paying attention to me being able to do everything.

So he redirected his attention to me and said, "Where have you been a surgical assistant before?"

My reply was simple. "I have never been a surgical assistant, this is my first time doing this," I said.

"No!!!" he said. "That's not true; I don't believe you. How do you know everything that we do? How do you know what everything is? How do you know how to rap the suture? How do you...?"

I said to him, "Doctor... I watch you every day. Whenever you guys were in here, when we left to go home, you never noticed that your surgical book was missing? Did you know I was reading the Merck manual at home, learning about different procedures and things like that? Did you not know that I was studying the instruments that I sterilized every time you guys did a surgery?"

The doctor was blown away, and he said, "You're better than my freaking nurses!"

All of this happened because I took the initiative to be the best at whatever it is I was going to be; because whatever I was, I wanted to be better than that and I wanted to grow in life.

How many of you go the extra mile at your job? How many times have you been put in a learning position or finished your work and was given an opportunity to learn someone else's job and you did not take it? Or you had a break or a lunch, and instead of going to lunch, you went to another section and just watched?

How many of you go home – and now Google has everything that you need to know– how many of you go home and google how they do whatever it is you do for work, how they make their car parts or how they put their car parts together if you work for a car manufacturer? If you work for a hospital, have you found out how certain procedures work? Or what happens if this patient has this? What are the outcomes? What could they possibly have? What could be possibly wrong with them? How many of you really go the extra mile and learn what it is that you're hired to do?

When you take the time to learn what it is that you're doing a step further, you become an asset to that company. Companies don't fire assets, they fire liabilities; they fire people that don't show up to work early. I showed up to work, believe me or not, I showed up to work early, thirty to fifty minutes early every day before I had to do work because I didn't know what would happen for sure; I never took it for granted that there wasn't going to be a car accident on the freeway and that I might be delayed.

I was late to my second job and they didn't allow anyone else to come in late, so that was totally different but what I'm saying is, every job that I had, I would go to work early, and I would learn or study someone else's job or watch somebody work or do something extra. When somebody called in ill for work, I would say; call me up. People called in all the time, being sick, showing up late; eventually, they got fired, and when they got fired, that was my time to shine.

Chapter 8

WHEN THEY GOT FIRED, I'd be there talking to the manager or the supervisor and informing them, "If somebody cancels or calls in, I can do overtime. I'll take forty hours plus."

I volunteered for forty hours plus because everybody knows that in overtime, when you go over forty hours you get what? Time and half.

One thing I can tell you from my overtime jobs is, don't do too much overtime, hahaha, because one time I did like eighty hours in a week and my check was like just, few hundred dollars more than it was regularly because Uncle Sam took most of it in taxes.

So once again, that was a learning experience for me, right? Yes, I worked overtime but not too much that Uncle Sam would take half of the check. In the eighty hours that I worked, I was supposed to get eight hundred, and I only got four hundred because Uncle Sam took the other four hundred. This is normal and of course, you get it back at the end of the year, which is a good thing too, but I wanted my money right then because I wanted to be able to save my own money, I didn't want Uncle Sam to make interest on my money, I wanted to add interest to my own money. Hahaha!!

You see, back then, I also invested in C.D.'s. C.D.'s had like a five to eight percent interest rate, so I put money into C.D.'s which grew my money faster. Now, we have something called bitcoin, a form of cryptocurrency. I started investing in that.

So, what I'm saying in essence is that when you become an asset, your job values you and when you become an asset and your job starts valuing you, they start calling you, giving you overtime. And when you don't show up, they lose interest in you and they start giving hours to other people, and then you start complaining when you look at your bank account, and you're like, I have no money.

Well, you don't have any money because you're doing nothing to get it. So, you have to sacrifice in order to grow. Sacrifice and do the overtime; sacrifice is key to success. I was a working magnet, I worked two jobs, and in between that on my days off, I did go to school and take those little classes that I told you about.

Sometimes, I would go to school like very early in the morning, and then, I would go to my job a little late. I don't know how I did that, but I did it. It definitely had something to do with my focus because I didn't go hanging out. After work, I came home and I studied or came home and rested because when I went to work, I needed to have all my brain cells functioning properly, so I needed the proper amount of rest.

So, I usually got off at eleven-thirty at night, and by the time I got home, it was twelve-thirty. I would sleep until about five-thirty, get up, get dressed, shower, and head back to work.

The first job I had wasn't that far from where I lived, so that worked out great and helped me stay focused. But I'm just saying, regardless of the circumstances, have a plan, have a goal, have a mission; otherwise, success is just a word that will never manifest, and it will never manifest because you're not doing anything towards manifesting it.

You can't just work on an idea or something that you want to happen and then when the opportunities come for you to work towards that happening for you, you don't take them.

Opportunity comes to you by people, things, situations, and all types of ways, and you need to be ready at all times. You could be at a movie theater and meet somebody that is in your area of expertise or maybe the area that you're trying to move into is their area of expertise, but if you disregard them or ignore them, you might totally miss out. You should take the initiative sometimes and strike conversations with people or be open to being approached because these conversations could be opportunities to meet people that can mentor you or coach you.

Nobody succeeds in life without mentors; even basketball players, celebrities, and billionaires. What happens when you have a mentor or a coach? They inspire you and push you beyond the limits that you will be able to push yourself. That's the value of having a mentor or accountability coach.

When you're at a gym, if you just go to the gym by yourself, how long are you going to stay on the treadmill? An hour, maybe? But if you have a coach that says, "You're going to stay on the treadmill for an hour, then you're going to work out on the weights for fifteen minutes, you're going to do twenty reps over here, you're going to do thirty reps." You might think like, "How in the world? I'm tired, my legs hurt," but you are very likely to finish the programs.

Your coach will most likely say, "You are alright; you're not going to fall off," because once they push you,

you will get to your destination, your desired size."

This is the thing called life, and this is how it works: you have to choose. Life is a decision, a choice, and every decision and every choice that you make directs the path of where your life is going to end up.

Chapter 9

WHERE DO YOU WANT to see your life tomorrow?

When do you want to move into your greatness? Are you tired of being tired? Are you sick and tired of being you? Are you sick and tired of your current situation? When you get sick and tired of your situation, you're going to make a change. You're going to accept people into your life that are going to teach you things. And you will open your mind when you realize that nobody makes it in life alone.

The founders of Microsoft, Facebook, and other great organizations did not make it on their own. They all had business partners, people in their lives that collaborated with them and helped them get together and they listened to Warren Buffett and the other big gurus. They went and found mentors, and they went on to become extremely successful.

Everybody needs help to succeed, and if you don't accept help and constructive criticism, you will lose. Do not take constructive criticism as being picked on; do not take constructive criticism as a chance to play the victim.

Take constructive criticism as "I'm being made into my greatness, I am. This thing is making me great, I am."

Till this day, as old as I am, I was in a meeting the other night, and we had this session that we do, it's like a little mastermind and the lady that I did the session with, she said, "Do you mind if I give you constructive criticism?"

I said, "Go for it."

So she gave me her bit of constructive criticism and when she was done, did I get mad, feel all stupid like, "You're just trying to pick on me, why are you going to tell me that?"

Because that's the attitude of know-it-alls; know-it-alls are not doers, they are people that, because of their attitude, can be labeled as fools. Anybody that doesn't learn is a fool; anybody that doesn't accept wisdom and knowledge is a fool, and that's straight out of the Bible.

So, in order to move from the foolish path, you must be able to take constructive criticism. Constructive criticism is a movement towards your growth in life. Why would you want to take a test that somebody else took and passed? Find the shortcuts, learn from others that have made that mistake already, why make the same mistake when someone can teach you to do it better the first time???

Let me tell you, when I was young, I mean really young, like in elementary and junior high school, I hung out with my friends but when I went to their houses, guess who I was really hanging out with their parents, especially their moms and their grand moms. Why? I was strongly drawn to them and the reason I was drawn to them was because they were older and smarter than me; they had lived more years than me. What did they have to teach me? What could they tell me that could make me avoid making mistakes in my young life?

I learned that sacrifice helps a person succeed faster in life. Right now, I don't have to sacrifice anymore; now I can have a party whenever I want. I can literally party all day, every day. Now, I can hang out or travel or do whatever I want to do because I sacrificed back then.

So, because I didn't want to be held back by mistakes in life, I hung around older people. My friends used to always ask me, "Why are you hanging around my mom? Why are you hanging around my grandma?"

And I literally would say, "Because they're smarter than you. You're the same age as me; you might be a year or two older than me or a year or two younger than me, what can you teach me? What can you teach me about this thing called life? You're the same age with me, you're at the same level as me, I talk to your mom and grandma and hang out with your mom and grandma because they're smarter than you and I want to be educated. I want to be coached; I want to be mentored."

I wanted to be taught the right path, and I'm going to tell you, to this day, I still talk to a lot of people, a lot of my friends are much older than me. I have friends that are ten, fifteen years, or twenty years older than me. I keep them because they're smarter than me; they're more knowledgeable than me.

Note that there are also young people that you can learn more than a few things from. I know some young people that are like in their thirties; they're just killer smart because the education that they're getting in college now, is way more advanced than what we were getting when we were young. So, I listen to some of them too because some of them come out with a great wealth of knowledge.

Some young adults drop out of college, by that I mean, they don't even finish college and they're millionaires because of what they're teaching them. You see? So, yes, by all means, listen to someone that's more knowledgeable than you, especially if that someone's doing what you want to do in life. With this attitude, you can grow and do what they do after watching and asking questions.

You will be able to gain something, but if you're a know-it-all, you will run into a lot of problems. Believe me; nobody wants to work with a person that thinks they know everything. Nobody.

Some people are quick to say, "I know how to do that!"

You might want to train them to do something or show them how to do something, and then they come to you and say, "Hey!!! I already know how to do that," and then you turn around and they aren't doing it right. Really!!

I thought you said you knew how to do it? Word of advice; don't say you know how to do something you don't know how to do because from that moment, you will be held accountable. From that moment, if I were in charge, I'd be looking at you with crossed eyes; I'd be looking to see if I want you to stay in my firm or if I'm going to fire you now. This is mostly because I'm only going to tell somebody one time or two times and explain it to them so they clearly understand what it is that their job description is, but when you don't allow that to happen, you lose if you mess up, all because you didn't pay attention; you're likely to get dismissed.

It's like that because business owners like to move on with their life because they really need to keep great ideas in their mind to grow their business. You feel where I'm going with this?

Chapter 10

SO, THIS IS THE mindset of successful business people – they are always ready to delegate activities. The mindset is to delegate it and get it off your list; that's why they call it delegating.

You have to learn it, do it, and delegate it. When another new activity comes up, learn it, do it, delegate it.

If you ever want to be a business owner, you have to know what your employees are doing; you have to know how your system works that you built to run that business because you want to run a business, you don't want to work a job.

Self-employment is called a job but you work for yourself, and you are at that business every day. You have to show up at that business every day, and if you don't show up every day, then that business is not going to function, that's self-employment.

I like creating businesses. A business is a functional place; a place that you can create your systems, put them in play and then you can be away, if and when you want.

The beauty of it all is that your business can function if you are in

China or if you're in Italy. You could be traveling the world and your business is still going to be operating, you're still going to be getting money.

How do you think C.E.O.s function? This is how C.E.O.s function: they go in, check in, check around, see what's being done, what they need to do, read a couple of documents, have a couple of meetings with the staff managers, and boom!!! They're out, they're gone. This doesn't mean they're not still working behind the scene to grow their company and their business, but they're not doing a ten dollar an hour job. You feel me? You understand where I'm going with this?

So, you don't want to put yourself in a position to work ten dollars an hour position, in your own business.

My mentor teaches me that anything that pays fifteen dollars an hour or less is not worth your time. Delegate it out; give it to somebody else because if you do it, you're wasting your time. You should have the mind of a genius, the mind of successful business people; you shouldn't have the mind of a nine to fiver, the mentality of a person working a J. O. B and be a business owner.

Being just over broke is not your destiny; that's not your goal, that's not your dream. In order to reach higher heights, you have to delegate the little things out. Okay!!

Now, every business has a system in place. A lot of business owners open a business, and they try to keep everything on paper. They have things written down, they have a little business plan and, they just go in and start working in their business. They don't have policies and procedures; they don't have any real systems in place. This is usually the problem with many business owners because systems are the key to success. If you can learn it, do it and delegate it, then your system works. It doesn't matter what kind of business you're in, you have to create a system for your business, and this is how your business will function when you're not around.

McDonalds, for example, has a system. Every McDonalds you go to, the French fries are always on the same side. Where is the distribution where they take the hamburgers and the wrapper? On the right. Where is the milkshake machine? On the right. Where is the coffee machine? On the left by the drive-through window.

How do I know all this? Because I pay attention to systems, I'm system-driven. Every successful business has systems, and that business is only as good as the system that drives it. My property management company, my property leasing company, and my hair salons all had systems.

If I didn't want to go to work at my leasing company, I didn't have to because I had people there that I delegated to.

I delegated to my secretaries and other members of my staff. So, when my son had a basketball game, guess where I was. At the basketball game. Was my office still functioning?

Absolutely. Was I still making money? Absolutely. Did I have to be there? No.

I don't even remember ever missing one of my son's games. Whatever events he had, we did everything together. Horseback riding, baseball, flag football, and most of all, basketball! My son really loved basketball. He was actually extremely good, but he was really short. Still, it was to his advantage to be short because while every other person else was tall on the court, I told him to just go through their legs. Hahaha. He was one heck of a defensive player, and I was there to witness it all; I was there with him at every game.

When he was younger, I went with him on every field trip. I think maybe I missed a couple, but for the most part, I was on every field trip with my son.

How many of you are missing that family-oriented lifestyle? Are you missing family time and missing those precious moments? It doesn't have to be that way!

Don't get it wrong; I was actually very busy. Did I have time to be one hundred percent in my son's life? No, I was a single mother trying to make it, trying to survive, trying to provide for my son so that he would never be without anything. So, did I give a hundred percent? No, but was I there at those valued moments? Was I there when he was performing on stage at his school event? Yes. Was I there when he was baptized? Yes. Was I there when he sang in that choir? Yes, I was there.

How many people have the chance and the opportunities to be there for their children? It's called a life of freedom. Success, financial stability, that's what it's called. It's also called being there when you are needed to be, at the important times. My mom didn't really have it easy. She moved to California with three kids and was barely surviving. We were just over broke but my oldest brother stepped in, and he took care of my brother and me. He was only what? Maybe twelve but he took care of us.

My mom did all she had to do to provide for us until my dad was able to get a transfer and come out there and join us. My mom provided for us, and it was mostly a struggle. I don't remember it so much, but there were many struggles. Still, when I had a ballet recital, was my mom there? Yes. When I had a performance on stage, was my mom there? Yes.

When I needed costumes, my mom didn't have the money to buy it, so my mom would make my costume and everybody else's costume and get paid for making their costumes. My mom was really an entrepreneur.

See, sometimes in life, especially when we are young, we go through things. We hardly ever understand what it is we're going through and why we're going through it. I thought my childhood was horrible, which it was. There were a lot of things I went through in my childhood, which I don't care to discuss but was I abused? Absolutely. Did my family abuse me? No. Did outsiders abuse me? Yes. Was I mentally, verbally, and physically abused? Yes, yes. It tore me up as a kid because I didn't know how to handle it; I didn't know what to do.

My parents had no other choice but to take me to counseling. Eventually, when I turned about twenty-five years, I sat back and thought about things, then went to my parents and told them how grateful and thankful I am for them because of the things that I despised about them, but which they didn't stop doing. They kept telling me what to do, being bossy, fussing at me, telling me, "Don't do this, don't do that, this is going to happen, that ain't going to happen, you're going to grow up and be nothing."

All these words rang loudly in my ears, and I was like, "Oh my god!!! You're getting on my nerves."

Strangely, my friends' mothers could tell me anything, and I'd listen. That's just a part of growing up. Every parent knows this truth: your teenager doesn't listen to you, they listen to everybody else other than you, but do they come back to the parents? Absolutely.

Did I come back to my parents? I did. I came back to my parents, and I told them, "I'm so happy and grateful that you raised me the way that you raised me. I'm so happy and grateful that when my friends at school had a leather coat and I came home and said, "Dad, can you buy me a leather coat? Everybody has a leather coat." He said, "You want a leather coat? Get a job and buy your own leather coat."

I thanked my dad for all the invaluable lessons although, at the time, I thought he was being mean. My dad didn't pay for my prom; I had to work and pay for my own prom. What kind of dad does that? I mean I'm his daughter. He didn't get me a prom car, didn't get my dress, didn't get my hair done; I had to collaborate to get things done. My mom and my aunt made my dress, my mom did my hair, and the lady down the street did my nails. Was I thankful? Yes. Could I focus on what he didn't do for me and spoil my prom? Yes, but did I do that? No.

Chapter 11

I ENDED UP GETTING everything I needed because of patience and perseverance, and it was a great lesson, even if I didn't get it at the time. Sometimes, we can't see where we're being led in life, but I just want to remind everybody, if you don't have anybody in your ear, you don't have anybody that loves you. If there isn't anybody telling you about the rights and wrongs of life, you have no love in your life.

When you have people telling you in your ear, they're telling you because they love you, they're telling you because they see the greatness within you, they're telling you that because they want to help you, they want to see the best for you; they want you to excel in life. They're not trying to tear you down but only trying to build you up. But if you don't have anybody in your ear, my heart goes out to you because that means you have no source of strength in your life. If nobody talks to you, you don't have anybody that cares enough to train you in the way that is right. When people are willing to talk in your ear, believe me, that's love, that's pure love right there. Today, I just want you to walk away with one thing. If I haven't taught you or educated you or put knowledge into your mind or your body or your soul concerning something that you didn't already know, so be it, but when the student is ready, the teacher will appear.

So when you are ready to step into your greatness, you don't have to worry, fret, try to figure it out or try to do anything at all. As you step into your greatness, the teacher that's supposed to take you there is going to show up, don't worry. And when they eventually show up, you can't reject it; you have to be ready.

So, you prepare in advance for the opportunity that you haven't seen that's coming your way but when it arrives, you need to be ready. So, whatever your dreams and your goals are, I want you to be ready for that opportunity, so prepare yourself.

When I wanted to write a book, someone asked me; why do you want to write a book? What's the book going to do? How are you going to make money off the book? Do you know that by merely telling that person about my book, they killed my dream for a moment because I started second-guessing myself and asking myself, "Well, why do I want to write a book? What is a book going to do for me?"

The book that I second-guessed myself about is the book that you're reading right now or listening to on audio tape. It's the same book that I told someone that did not see my vision or my dreams and discouraged me from moving forward, thereby holding me back for a short time. Had I stayed in that zone, you would not be reading this book and/or listening to this audio right now.

Therefore, I ask you to follow your dreams, follow your goals. What you want wants you, and it's just waiting for you do open that door and ask. Every word you speak, every phrase that you speak, is a prayer request to God and the universe for what you want. Speak life into yourself. Do not speak grime, dirt, discouragement, frustration or hatred into your life. Look yourself in the mirror every morning and tell yourself how great you are because you are great!

If you haven't been aware of this technique or used it before now, your life may not be going the way you want, but the moment you start looking in the mirror and proclaiming greatness, greatness will follow. I know because I've been there. I never used to practice it, but at some point, I began to stand in the mirror and say, "Yvette, you are greater than what you are complaining about. You are greater than your obstacles. You are greater than these losers that are telling you that you're dreaming. Your vision is going to come to pass."

Just like me, you need to tell yourself that you are greater than obstacles. The words, "I am that, I am!" are powerful. The "I am" is huge. When you speak 'I am' into your life, you speak God and the universe into your life, so whatever you say after I am comes to pass. Using just those two words is a life changer. You can Google it or YouTube it to confirm.

Those two words, in combination, are probably the greatest words in this world and Bible with the power to change lives, manifest anything that you want, and speak life into yourself.

If you're constantly telling yourself that you hate yourself, you don't like yourself, you are horrible and that nobody likes you, guess what; people are going to keep coming into your life that won't like you, will hate you and make you feel horrible.

Start speaking the opposite; say, "I am love, I am light, I am likable, I'm funny, I'm patient, I'm kind, I'm gentle."

Speak those things that are not, as if they were, and they shall come to pass.

Now, you can speak good, or you can speak bad, it doesn't matter; the universe and God can't tell whether you want it or you don't want it, when you feel it, it shows in your emotion. If you have joyful, happy emotions are going to come to you. It's more than just the word but it starts with the word because the word creates the emotion and the emotion creates the feeling and then the universe knows that you're feeling phenomenal or you're feeling good and it brings more things to you that make you feel good, make you feel better, make you have more joy and more happiness.

It's a fact that bad things are going to happen in life. Life is going to hit you hard, but like my dad told me, it's not how hard you fall; it's how hard you get back up.

I have something that I call the twenty-four hour incubation period, if

I'm mad or frustrated or something is not going right, things are just not working for me, I will go and I will cry. I will be depressed, I will lie on my bed with my covers over on my head, I might drink a beer to go to sleep, and I'm not even a drinker. I'm going to do whatever I need to do to get away from that situation for a moment and feel why I am feeling this way. I'm going to feel everything I'm feeling fully; I'm not going to suppress anything because that makes depression and anxiety come out.

I'm going to feel everything; I'm going to cry, I'm going get my pillow and scream in it. I'm going to do whatever I need to do. I'm going to cry all day, all night if I want to, but in twenty-four hours, I will get up, I will shake it off and I'm coming back twice as hard because my dad told me there are no losers in our family, there are no weak people in our family. We are strong, we overcome every obstacle and every challenge, and if you show me weakness, I will show you things that you never thought you could see, but if you want love, joy, and happiness, you will get exactly what you put out. But you never fall weak, never, no matter what happens to you, you never feel sorry for yourself because you didn't deserve that, you didn't just necessarily deserve it, it was a lesson that you had to learn, that's a lesson.

The more obstacles, the more trials, the more tribulations that you have, the stronger you will be. And the more connected you are with God and the universe, the more purpose you have in your life. People that don't have any purpose are the people that are out there doing bad things, committing crimes, because they have no purpose. They don't see success, they don't change their life, and they end up dead or in jail eventually, because karma does come back and bite you. They see a short term victory, only a short term victory but the struggle, the sacrifice, the trials and tribulations come to those who endure it.

I used to ask God, "God can I get a break?" and I heard Him say, "No."

I said, "Why not?"

He said, "Because you are stronger than your obstacles and I know you're not weak, you will get back up, I gave that test because I knew that you could pass it. Why will I give you a test that I know you're going to fail?"

God is not a failing God, right? He can't make our decisions and choices, but He doesn't want to see you fail. He wants you to step into your greatness. Sometimes, trials are hard, but if you have faith and you believe, that's all you need, faith and belief of a mustard seed. You will survive! You're going to get through it, and you're going to look back and be like, "What?!!! I got through that? I can't believe that I went this far. Oh my God!!! This happened to me in my life, and then I got through it."

Chapter 12

YOU NEED TO STOP looking at your failures and start looking at your successes; whether they are big or small, you need to start acknowledging them. Give yourself some credit, pat yourself on the back, you don't need other people to do it for you. The only approval you need is the approval of God and yourself, that's it. Everybody else's opinions and thoughts don't matter. They can't see your dream, they can't see your vision, and so they may not like what you produce.

For instance, this book, I know some people won't like it. Do you think I care? No! Because the ones that need it will like it; when the student is ready, the teacher will appear. If you don't like it, go buy another book, go buy another audio. It's fine with me. I wish you much love and blessings in your life.

Can we please everybody? No, we can't. Do most people live their lives trying to please other people? Yes, they do. I was one of those people, so I know. I can't teach you anything that I haven't experienced. How can I be passionate and tell you the truth of something I have never experienced?

I have had multiple trials and tribulations combined within my life. They weren't pretty when I was going through it, trust you me, it was hard to wake up every day, it was hard to take another breath, it was hard!!

To illustrate, I'm going to tell you this quick story, and I'm going to let you go. There was a young man that met a millionaire, and he said, "Sir, would you be my mentor and coach me? I want to know how you became a millionaire; can you teach me how you became a millionaire?"

The millionaire told him, "Meet me at the beach tomorrow morning at five o'clock a.m."

So the young man meets the millionaire at the beach, thinking they were going to chill out and he's going to be talking to him, telling him this long story, whatever.

The millionaire says, "Walk out in the water."

The young man is surprised. "What, walk out in the water?" he asks.

"Yes," the millionaire replies. "Walk out in the water."

The young man walks out to the water to the point where the water is to his waist.

"Go deeper in the water," the millionaire says.

"What?" the young man exclaims. "It's five o'clock in the morning; it's cold."

"Go deeper in the water," the millionaire says, assuredly.

The young man walks deeper into the water and in no time, it is at his neck.

The millionaire says, "Keep walking," and the young man keeps walking until the water is at his chin.

"Okay man," the young man says, "this is getting a little interesting. Why am I walking in this cold water at five o'clock in the morning? This is not teaching me how you became a millionaire; I want to know how you became a millionaire. Why exactly am I in the ocean?"

The millionaire walks out to the ocean and stands close to young man as the water stays level at his chin. The millionaire pushes the young man's head under the water and holds him down.

The young man kicks and fights as he tries to get out and get some air.

The rich man keeps holding the young man's head down in the water until he starts to lose energy and starts kicking.

At that moment, the rich man lets him up, and the young man coughs violently as he tries to speak. "Why did you do that?" "Are you trying to kill me? I don't want you to kill me; I wanted to just know how you became a millionaire."

The millionaire says, "Let me ask you a question; when your head was under that water, how bad did you want to breathe?"

The young man said, "I wanted to breathe really bad."

"How hard did you fight to come up for that breath of air?" the millionaire asks. "Did you give it all you had to push against my strength from holding you down in that water? Did you give it all you had?"

The young man says; "I gave it everything I had and then finally just had peace."

The millionaire tells him, "That's how I became a millionaire. I wanted it so bad that it was like taking my last breath on earth. The pain was so intense and so many obstacles and things along my journey but I wanted it so bad."

You have to know; you know you're 'why.' You have to know why you want that success. You got to know why you want that destiny, that outcome. Is your 'why' sufficient enough to get you through the things and the challenges that you're going to encounter on your way to that destination. Your 'why' has to be strong. What's your reason for wanting to get there? That's what's going to take you there because nothing can stop you if your 'why' is strong. Nothing, nobody, no obstacle, no dream killers can stop you.

Some of you want to have children, some of you want to live in another country, some of you want a big house or a little car or some of you just want to serve, you want to be able to travel to other countries such as me and just serve other people. Your 'why' has to be big enough to get you there. If you don't have a reason and a 'why' that you want to get there, there will be a big problem. Remember that your 'why' cannot be money driven, it can never be money driven.

Oprah Winfrey said these words years ago. I'll never forget this and people state this all the time. "If you do your passion, the thing that it is that you love the most in this life, the money will follow." It has to be a passion, and once you're passionate about it, the money will flow. Never work for money, you'll stay broke. Never! You'll stay broke because money is working you. Switch the role?

Work because you love what you're doing for work. Even if you don't love your job, make yourself, feel and be comfortable in your job because you could love your job even though you don't like your job, you should know this, it's all in your mind! You create your reality in your mind. So, if you tell yourself enough you don't like the job, guess what, you're not going to like that job.

Start telling yourself, "I'm so happy and grateful I have a job, I'm so happy and grateful I have money coming in every day, I'm so happy and grateful that oh my God!!! This is such a blessing to have a job because so many people don't have jobs." Be grateful, watch more great things come into your life, more prosperity, more things, more good things are going to come into your life. Life is all what you make it, it can be great or it can be sad. Your choice, your decision! With that being said, this is Miss Yvette Live; you all have a phenomenal day. Bye for now!

Recap of the lessons:

- Being an asset at your job or position!

- Going beyond a job to become a business owner!

- Learning how to implement a system in your business!

- Mastering the system and delegating little jobs to others!

- Learning the importance of collaborations to business success!

- Don't let money work you, work your passion!

- Know your Why!

- How to sacrifice for your dreams and future!

- Work like a millionaire to become one!

- Feel the pain, to reap the rewards!

- Always have an Accountability coach!

" Dare to be different, and let your light shine"
"Move swift, stay humble!"
- Ms.Yvette

Send a TEXT to **39492**, MESSAGE **"Inspire101"** For updates on upcoming books and online training courses.

Contact me for speaking engagements, coaching, and book permissions, at sales@succeedwithmsyvette.com

Book Reviews are appreciated, please leave a Great review, if you found value or were inspired by my lessons. :)

About the Author

YVETTE, has been a Serial Entrepreneur for 30 years. Has experience in the Health care industry, Beauty industry, most areas of Real Estate, including rehabbing, sales, and leasing.

New ventures include, being a New Author, Teaching and coaching others to an even greater level of success.

Working with new and seasoned Entrepreneurs. Together we start from the inside to guarantee the success on the outside. Entering the

thinking process and creating systems
to ensure the level of success we are
striving for in any area of their lives.

As a business owner coaching teams
and staff to obtain mental awareness
of how thoughts equal results.
Inspiring others to bring out their
greatness, to achieve any goal or
mission they see fit to accomplish. It
all starts with you!

When others succeed, I succeed with
accomplishing my purpose on the
Earth! Serving others!!

Wishing you much Happiness and
Success, because you deserve it!
God Bless! Namaste!

Yvette Hebert

www.ingramcontent.com/pod-product-compliance
Lightning Source LLC
Chambersburg PA
CBHW061536050726
47593CB00002B/806